Pillow
with a
Heartbeat

Nancy Stanley and Truffles

Journey Publishing · Carlsbad CA

www.PillowWithAHeartbeat.com

ISBN-13: 978-09817069-1-7

Second Edition: March, 2011

To Michelle Butler, who at the age of sixteen maintained a spirit that captured all that is beautiful and good throughout her difficult journey with cancer.

With her amazing spirit and her passion for life, she taught me that without faith, love, and hope we cannot realize the true gift of living.

Because of her, I have learned to open my heart to those who will let me in.

Thank you, Michelle.

Contents

Thank you!

Acknowledgments

I give my fullest gratitude to Nancy Hardin for her wise editorial guidance. Because of her love for dogs, she was the perfect person to get inside Truffles' head and see his vision.

Thank you to Andrew Chapman, for helping me design such a beautiful cover that looks like eye candy.

To my wonderful Mother who constantly encourages me to pursue my dreams. I would not be the person I am today if I did not have her to emulate.

To my children and my beautiful grandchildren, who fill my world with love, pride and joy, and who make me want to pay it forward for all they give to me.

And last but not least, to "Truffles", my five pound poodle, who has a lion's heart and an angel's soul. I thank him every day for sharing his devotion and his loving licks with everyone he meets, especially the children. He makes this world a brighter place!

Be the kind of person that your dog
thinks you already are.

Introduction

I wrote this story for every dog lover in the world who wants to say thank-you to "Fido" or "Fifi" for loving them unconditionally and for getting them through times of sadness and loneliness.

Had I not had my dog years ago when my parents divorced, my life would have taken a completely different turn. He was my rock and my comfort during that time, and my best friend. He never judged or ridiculed me and he listened to whatever I had to say, night and day. He licked away my tears and made me laugh with his antics. He was everything to me.

So remember to thank your dog every day for teaching you the real meaning of love; and try to be the kind of person that your dog thinks you already are.

Now, to let Truffles tell his story …

I miss my mommy.

Chapter 1
A Rough Start

Being born so tiny wasn't really a lot of fun. I'm a boy and my three sisters were all bigger and fatter than I was. Sometimes I felt invisible. If they weren't pretending that I wasn't even there, they were ganging up on me and sitting on my head, or all nipping at me at once. Maybe these were signs of affection. If they were, I didn't like them, but I wasn't big enough to defend myself, so I had to put up with it.

Whenever it was time to eat, Mommy would roll over on her back and my sisters would tumble over each other to get to her as fast as they could. "Now, now, girls," she would say. "Give the baby a turn."

But I had to wait for them to drink all they wanted of Mommy's milk before I could manage to get even one sip. When it was finally my turn, I was in heaven. Mommy always let me stay for as long as I wanted. I drank slowly just to stay close to her. She was so warm and soft. I could feel her love for me and, snuggled up next to her, I thought what a lucky puppy I was.

As I drank, Mommy's tongue licked me everywhere I had a place to lick. It was a special bath and I think maybe she gave it to me because I was the tiniest of her babies. I also think that Mommy was happy that I was a boy. Her only boy. Maybe that's why my sisters picked on me.

When I was done drinking my milk, I looked like a pot-belly pig. My tummy was so full that it touched the ground when I tried to walk. It got in my way. Being only a couple of weeks old, I couldn't walk all that well yet anyway.

What I loved most was falling asleep to the sound of Mommy's heartbeat. That soft "thump, thump, thump" was my lullaby. It was a sound that made me feel safe. It meant love to me then, and it still does.

After a few weeks, I was getting bigger. I weighed about twelve ounces and I could almost run without tripping over my own paws. It was so exciting to be able to keep up with my sisters. Pretty soon they stopped teasing me and after that we all had fun playing together. Now I loved my family!

Then one day, Mommy startled me by suddenly running all around our pen, barking and crying. She grabbed me by the

"Please, you can't take my baby. He's too small and he still needs me to feed him. Please don't take him."

neck and pulled me close to her as she backed away from the lady who was coming toward us and looking straight at me.

"Please, you can't take my baby. He's too small and he still needs me to feed him. Please don't take him. He's not strong enough yet. I won't let you take him."

She was whimpering and trying with all her might to stop the lady from lifting me up out of the pen. It was no use. In a flash, I was so high off the ground that I felt dizzy and sick. As the lady carried me away from my family, I squirmed around in her arms so I could look back. I could see Mommy lying there, exhausted, with my frightened sisters huddled around her. She howled as she watched me disappear. I had no idea what was happening, or why.

I was put in a room where I was surrounded by a bunch of puppies, lying still and crying or yipping and jumping all around. There were no soft blankets to lie on, only newspapers spread on the floor. I was so scared that I started to tremble.

Who would snuggle with me and keep me safe at night? Who would feed me warm milk and clean my eyes and ears? Why did the lady put me in here? I could still hear my mommy crying, and I couldn't go to her or help her. I couldn't help me. I longed to hear her heartbeat lullaby so I could fall asleep. Instead, I was alone with the sound of the other puppies crying.

There were so many puppies in the room. They were all different colors and sizes but I think we were all poodles because that's what I heard the lady call us. Some were black and white, some brown and white; and some were even red, and apricot. There was one puppy that looked just like me. When I first saw him, I thought I was in two places at one time. Apparently we were both "chocolates." I didn't know it at the time but being a chocolate would turn out to be a blessing for me.

That puppy and I were the same age and smaller than all the other dogs. As soon as he saw me, he scrambled over to my side and plopped down as close to me as he could. We looked at each other and knew right away that we would be friends. For some reason I thought he needed me even more than I needed him and that made me feel good. It made me feel like a big brother and I liked the feeling.

Although I kept on missing my mommy, I spent lots of time with my new friend. It turned out that he had been ripped away from his family the same way I had been. We pretended to be brave but oh, how we missed our mommies. We shared our food and water and we cuddled together to stay warm. As the days passed and we got even bigger, we mastered the art of running and jumping by play-ing together. One of our favorite games was to each hold one end of a toy and have a tug of war. We growled as fiercely as we could

We growled as fiercely as we could with our squeaky little voices, seeing who could sound the scariest.

with our squeaky little voices, seeing who could sound the scariest. When we were playing like that, we would forget to be lonely.

Sometimes we played so hard that we conked out and then we would sleep for hours. We did a lot of sleeping, but so did all of the other puppies. He and I didn't leave each other's side for one minute, except to make pee and poop on the newspapers. It was always pretty dirty in the room. We had a hard time finding a clean spot to go on and often ended up stepping in some other puppy's mess. I hated being so dirty. I would think of my mommy and how she had kept me so clean and so happy. But he and I licked each other's fur and tried to make the best of it.

Even though I was pretty happy a lot of the time I was with him, I still missed my mommy. I dreamed of her at night and I would wake up to find I'd been crying in my sleep. None of us puppies were ever held or cuddled. The lady didn't even have time to keep us as clean as we should have been. Only when people came to look at us would she give us each a quick once-over and fluff us up, but we were dirty the rest of the time.

I didn't like it when strangers picked me up. No one did it the right way. Sometimes they lifted me up by the skin of my neck and let my legs just hang. Mommy used to pick me up that way but when she did it, it didn't hurt and I wasn't frightened. What I really wanted to say to them was "Please hold me closer so I can hear your heart beat." (I had discovered that I could tell everything I needed to know about people by listening to their heartbeat.) But they never did.

Every time new people came, a puppy would disappear from the pen. I would think, "Please don't let my best friend disappear!" He and I would try to hide so no one would see either one of us and try to separate us. We decided that we were even more than just friends, we were brothers, and we swore to protect each other the way that brothers do.

One hot summer day, my friend and I were together in the yard outside the pen. Now that all of us were bigger and more grown up, we would be let out of the pen a few times a day, especially when people came to look us over. That day, a lady and a man sat down and started playing with my friend. I kept thinking, as hard as I could, "Please don't like him. Please don't take him!" I ran around trying to bark, but my bark wasn't loud enough to distract them. So I tried whimpering but they didn't seem to notice me, no matter what I did.

My friend sat very quietly at first, looking at them and sizing them up. Then his tail started wagging and he was licking their faces. He could tell that he was the one they had chosen to adopt, and so could I. He seemed so happy! Soon they were both kissing him and passing him back and forth to each other, holding him so close that I was sure he could hear their hearts beating.

Really scared by now, I stopped whining and went over to them, wagging my tail. Maybe they would like me too and take both of us. But it was no use. They got up off the floor and the man held my best—my only—friend and talked softly to him, while the lady filled out some papers. They already had a name for him, "Tanner," and they were calling him that. I was repeating, over and over again, "Please don't go. I want to come with you. I will miss you so much. Please don't disappear." But he didn't seem to hear me.

And then he was gone. Once again, I was alone. I couldn't understand why they hadn't liked me. What was wrong with me? I was a chocolate, just like him, and I was a boy, too.

> *I fell asleep thinking of my mommy. She was gone and now my best friend, my brother, was also gone.*

I fell asleep thinking of my mommy. She was gone and now my best friend, my brother, was also gone. I was so depressed I couldn't eat. I had no one to play with. I didn't even have a name of my own, like Tanner now had. I so wanted to be with Tanner and his new family.

Every now and then I would wonder about my father. I don't really know who he is, but I know he's a chocolate poodle, just like me. There are not too many of us around and I think he travels around to visit lots of mommy dogs so there will be more of us. The lady tells people that he's famous, and that he has perfect lines and that he's tiny, like me. It would be nice to meet him some day, but since I don't know him, I don't really miss him. It's my mommy that I miss and want to be with again.

Chapter 2
A New Mom

A few days later I woke up to lots of noise. People were running frantically back and forth and puppies were yelping. I hid in a corner of my pen, shaking with fright from all the commotion. What could be going on? Why were people shouting, "What are we going to do? Hurry and get the doctor here!"

The lady came over to the pen and picked up three of the puppies. She handled them very carefully and tears were in her eyes. I had never seen her hold any of us like that. Then I noticed that the puppies she'd picked up were not moving. Their eyes were closed as if they were sleeping, in spite of all the noise. A few minutes later, she put them in a box and took them away. Were they going to put me a box, too?

I was never as afraid as I was at that moment. All that I

could think of was how lucky Tanner was to be away from here and with those nice people, where he was safe. I pictured him curled up in a clean bed lined with soft blankets. I imagined his new mom and dad making sure he had everything he needed. Lucky Tanner! I rolled myself up into a little ball and trembled myself to sleep.

I never saw the puppies they took away in the box again. It turned out that some of our food had contained rat poison and the puppies that ate that food died. Because I hadn't been eating very well since Tanner left, I'd been put on a special diet and hadn't been given any of the bad food.

I never saw the puppies they took away in the box again.

For a while after I learned that, I felt that maybe I was lucky after all, like Tanner, and I even dreamed one night that Tanner and the nice man and woman who took him away came back to get me. But it was only a dream.

On one warm afternoon, all the puppies were outside in the sun. We couldn't play on the grass but we got to be on the terrace. It had a big fence around it and we could run around inside the fence all we wanted.

Not many people had come to see us that day, and since I still had no one to play with, I was sleeping in a patch of sunlight. I was awakened by two delicate hands gently lifting me up and holding me close. Before I even opened my eyes, I heard a strong, steady heartbeat. The woman who held me enveloped in her arms was beautiful. She kept looking at me with the most amazing smile. I wanted to say, "You are squeezing me a little too tight," but even if I couldn't breathe very well, it felt good to be held, so I just kept looking up at her without making a sound.

The lady stayed with me for a very long time. We were on the floor together and then I climbed into her lap and closed my eyes. I felt like everything was finally going to be all right.

At long last I had found a mom to love me. I wanted to share my good news with Tanner, but he wasn't there to tell.

By the time the lady put me back down into the pen, I was wagging my tail and jumping all around, like a rabbit. I was so excited at the thought of having a home with someone so nice. I was almost two months old now. I had waited a long time and now the waiting was over.

But then something went wrong. The beautiful lady with gentle hands was walking away from me. "Wait! Where are you going? No, please, don't you leave me, too! I want you to be my mom. Please take me away from here!"

As if she'd heard me, she turned around and came back. She picked me up again, gave me more kisses and hugs, and put me back down. And then she was gone, just like that.

How could she have left me? I couldn't stop crying. I would never ever have a family. I cried and cried and cried until finally I cried myself to sleep, wishing that I too had eaten the bad food and been taken away in a box.

A few weeks passed and it was beginning to seem as if I would be here forever. Lots of people were coming now but no one like the beautiful lady, no one whose heartbeat reminded me of my soft, furry mommy. I hated it when people turned me over on my back to see if I was a girl or a boy. I don't know why they couldn't just ask someone. I no longer had any hope of being chosen and to avoid any more disappointments, when I was picked up, I would stay very quiet. I wouldn't wag my tail to make them think I liked them. Sometimes I would even chew on their shoes. They would say things like, "I don't think we should take this one. He's awfully quiet and he's going to be a chewer." Then when they turned away I would secretly wag my tail just a little, knowing that I was not going to be going home with the wrong family.

In the pen, I was lonely. I still didn't feel like playing

with the other puppies. All I did was sleep and think about the beautiful lady and Tanner. I wondered if he missed me, too, wherever he was. It was getting harder and harder to remember my mommy, but the memory of her heartbeat stayed with me, strong as ever.

Then one morning I woke up to a familiar voice. At first I didn't want to open my eyes, in case I was dreaming. If it was a dream, I wanted to keep dreaming. It sounded like the beautiful lady's voice, but that wasn't possible. Or was it? Before I decided to open my eyes, I felt a pair of warm, soft hands lifting me gently up out of the pen and I knew I wasn't

At first I didn't want to open my eyes, in case I was dreaming. If it was a dream, I wanted to keep on dreaming.

dreaming. Someone was holding me very close. When I heard the heartbeat, I knew right away who it was. I was so excited that I could hardly breathe. I couldn't stop my tail from wagging. My whole body was wagging, I was so happy.

I looked up and saw her face. She had tears in her eyes, but they were happy tears. I licked her face as fast as I could. The tears were very salty. Even her arms were salty, so I kept licking and licking her all over. She seemed to like it because she was smiling and laughing at me. The beautiful lady had come back for me. I had found a mom.

I don't know why she left me the first time, but it didn't matter now. She'd come back! This time she didn't put me down for one second. She thanked the lady, wrapped me up in the softest of blankets, and took me outside and into a car, where she put me on her lap. As I was looking up at her, she said, "What a beautiful, tiny baby. You are my little pound of chocolate. I can't believe I'm taking you home. I love you so much, Truffles."

I didn't know what "Truffles" meant. It sounded like a funny name for a boy dog, but she could have called me "hey, you," for all I cared. The important thing was that now

I, too, had a name of my very own, and someone who cared enough to name me.

I fell fast asleep, dreaming of what my life was going to be like from now on. Even though I was happy to leave my pen, I felt sad that the other puppies were still in that dirty place waiting for someone to adopt them and not knowing if anyone ever would. But I cheered up at the thought that if it could happen to Tanner—and now, to me—then it could happen to them also.

Chapter 3
Coming Home

"Home at last!" My new mom parked her car in the garage and carried me into her house. Everything was so big and white and clean. The first room she took me to was filled with a gazillion toys, just for me. There were balls of every color and size, stuffed animals, bones to chew on and a fluffy bed to sleep in. I kept jumping around and rolling over and over with excitement. There were sweaters and jackets and a bunch of different colored leashes hanging on a hook by the door. On one table, there was a very big bowl filled with all kinds of chocolate treats. Apparently Mom loved chocolate. I think my being chocolate was why she chose me.

Mom carried me around for most of the rest of that day. At first I thought it was because she missed me if I left her side for even one minute. I knew how awful it felt to miss someone so I was very happy to be carried around. But it turned out that what Mom was doing was showing me around my new home, making sure that I felt secure everywhere before putting me down and letting me explore on my own. She thought that adjusting to a new place was going to be difficult for me but the minute I had settled into her lap riding home in the car, I had known that I wouldn't have to adjust to anything. I couldn't have felt more contented or loved.

There were big yellow pads on the floor in each room. Mom put me on one of them and explained, "This is where you make pee pee and poo poo until you are old enough to go outside, like the big dogs."

What did she mean, "old enough?" I was almost ten weeks old and I weighed one and one-eighth pounds! I felt totally ready to go outside, but I decided to be patient and go on the pee pee pads, just like she said. She was pleased that I caught on so fast. "You are the smartest little dog I have ever had, Truffles. I love you so much!"

As I ran around my new home, I realized that there was no way I could get from one floor to the next, without help. I sat looking up at a long flight of stairs that never ended. How was I supposed to climb up by myself? Mom looked at me sit-

Those stairs looked like a lot of fun and I wanted to try them on my own.

ting there and started to laugh. "What's the matter, Truff? Is my little boy too tiny to climb the stairs? In a few months you will be big enough to do it, but for now I will just have to carry you up and down. Don't worry."

I didn't want to wait. Those stairs looked like a lot of fun and I wanted to try them on my own. I backed way up, ran as fast as I could and then jumped. Whoops! I fell back down on my tush. I sat there, defeated and embarrassed.

Mom laughed and picked me up. "Patience, my little one. Patience."

It didn't take me long to settle into my new home. For a while, though, I had tummy aches sometimes. When I had a tummy ache, I didn't always get to the yellow pad in time. If Mom knew that I had really tried and that the mistake wasn't my fault, she didn't get upset with me. But when I got lazy once or twice and missed the paper because I didn't try hard enough to reach it, then I got a scolding. Those were the only times Mom ever got angry with me. I hated upsetting her and after a few times, I never did it again.

Mom and I spent hours on the floor, playing with my toys or just hanging out together. At first, when Mom threw a ball for me to fetch, I didn't know what "fetch' was so I just sat and looked at her. She laughed at me—she was always laughing at me—but I soon caught on.

She picked me up and I saw tears in her eyes. "I can't

believe how happy you make me. You've filled up such a big, lonely gap in my life." She kissed me and held me tight. I could feel both her sadness and her joy. I had figured out that the more I licked her, the more she smiled, so I licked her so much that my tongue got tired.

While we were playing one afternoon, the doorbell rang. The sound startled me and I barked. It wasn't a very big bark, but Mom said, "Good boy, Truffles. You are a terrific watchdog. How did you know to bark when the bell rings? You are just too smart!"

From then on, I barked whenever anyone came to the door. I liked being thought of as a "terrific watchdog."

Mom opened the door. There was a little boy standing there, with a huge smile on his face. He had big eyes and a golden tan. He wore overalls and a baseball cap turned around backwards. He was holding a delicious-looking bone in his hand. I had never seen such a bone and I started licking my lips. Mom picked him up, wrapping her arms around him. He hugged her and gave her a big kiss. "Hi, Darryl. How's my big boy doing today? Did you come to meet Truffles?"

The minute he saw me, he started squealing so loudly that I got scared. Mom asked him to try not to yell, since it obviously frightened me. He came over to me and started hugging me and rubbing my head. "Aww, what a cute puppy. You are so little. Look at those teeny feet. You look just like a little piece of chocolate. Did you know that you are Aunt Danny's favorite flavor?"

He had the kind of laugh that makes everyone around laugh, too. His laugh made my tail wag even more.

He and Mom laughed so hard. He had the kind of laugh that makes everyone around laugh, too. His laugh made my tail wag even more.

Darryl got very quiet then, and curled up with me on the floor for a long time. It turned out that he rubbed my ears just the way I liked, and held me near his chest so I could hear his heart beating. It was going fast and I could tell he was very excited to be with me. Finally, he got up and handed me the bone I'd had my eye on every since he came in. I crawled into his lap and chewed away. I had never had anything like that to chew on and it was yummy. It was so big that I couldn't even get my mouth around it, but I managed to get the meat off it anyway.

"Aunt Danny, can Truffles be my dog, too?"

Mom told Darryl that yes, I could be his dog, but that I would have to live with her. "You can come and visit Truffles any time you want, honey."

Darryl hugged her. "Oh, thank you, Aunt Danny. I can't wait to tell my friends at school. Can I bring Truffles in for show-and-tell?"

Mom told him that was a great idea, but not right away. "You need to wait until Truff is a little older and has had all his shots."

After that, Darryl came over almost every day to play with me. He lived just down the block so he was allowed to walk over after school. Whenever the bell rang and I knew he was at the door, my tail would start wagging uncontrollably. By then I had figured out that the happier I was, the faster it would wag.

"I'm not really feeling too good."

Chapter 4
Fighting Hard

One Friday afternoon, Darryl was visiting and planning to spend the night at our house. During the day I started coughing and my right ear began to hurt. I could tell Mom was worried about me. She felt my nose and said that it was a little warm, instead of cool and wet, the way it usually was. "What's the matter, Truffy? Do you have a fever? I think I'm going to have you looked at, to make sure you're okay."

She called the local vet and made an appointment for later that day. Darryl was getting upset. Tears welled up in his eyes. "Is Truffles going to die? Aunt Danny, don't let him die."

She told him that I would be fine and to think only good thoughts. "Positive thinking is very powerful, Darryl. We're going to make sure that nothing happens to our Truffles."

Darryl held me close and kept saying over and over, "I am positive you will be okay, Truffles. I am positive you are not going to die."

When we got to the vet's, we waited for a long time to be seen. When the doctor came out and called my name, there was something about him that I didn't like. My tail went down and I started to shake. He scared me and I didn't know why but I had a bad feeling. We went into a small room that had a big metal table in it. There was a funny smell in there that made me cling closer to Mom. I wanted to go home. Mom didn't put me down because she could tell I was scared. The doctor asked his assistant to take my temperature. I couldn't believe that they were going to put that thing into my tushie. I closed my eyes. Mom held me close and rubbed my ears and kissed the top of my head. Her soft voice kept saying, "It's okay, Truff. You're going to be fine. I love you, Truffles."

Darryl was standing up as tall as he could but he couldn't quite see over the table. "I'm here, too, Truff. Don't worry. I get that thing in my tush when I'm sick, and it doesn't hurt."

Mom told the doctor that I had been coughing and that my right ear seemed red. He took a look at it and gave her medicine for my ears. He told her that the cough was nothing to worry about. Then he said that I needed to be given my first puppy shots, and left the room to get them. When he came back, Mom asked him if he was sure I should get my shots when I wasn't feeling well. He assured her that it was fine. Mom wasn't convinced. "Maybe we could wait a week or so?"

The doctor insisted it was okay and all of a sudden I let out a yelp. The doctor had stuck me with a needle and it hurt. Darryl was upset, too. "He hurt Truffy, Aunt Danny!"

Mom told Darryl that sometimes shots hurt but it was over now and everything would be fine. We left the vet and went home.

After a few hours, my cough started to get worse. Later that night my neck and one of my legs hurt so badly that I began crying and couldn't stop. Every time I moved, it ached more. When I tried to stand up, I fell over. Mom looked as if she was going to cry, too. She could tell that something was very wrong. She called the doctor. His office was closed so she hung up, put Darryl to bed in the guest bedroom, then settled me on a heating pad on her bed and held me. After a few hours, I was so exhausted that I finally fell asleep but at three in the morning, I was coughing more than ever. I didn't want to eat or drink anything. I thought about being put in a box. I didn't want to die!

Mom was frantic. She called the doctor again and was told she would have to wait until he could be reached. Two hours went by before he called back. Mom told him what was going on. He insisted it was normal to have a reaction like that after the shots. Mom's voice got louder. "This is not normal! Truffles can't stand up. He won't eat or drink. His cough is terrible. I should never have let you give him those shots!"

He told her that she was overreacting and she hung up the phone. When she came back into the room, I must have looked pretty awful because she let out a cry. "Oh, my God, Truffles, what's the matter, baby?"

She picked me up. I was on fire. I had trouble seeing and I couldn't hold up my head. She called the Emergency Vet Clinic and they told her to come in right away. She wrapped me up in a blanket, woke Darryl, got him dressed and hurried us into the car. She couldn't stop shaking and crying—not happy tears but tears that scared me.

She couldn't stop shaking and crying – not happy tears but tears that scared me.

Darryl was still sleepy. "Where are we going, Aunt

Danny?" She told him that I had gotten worse and that we had to hurry to the hospital. I noticed that this time she didn't reassure him that I was going to be fine. She just hugged him, with tears rolling down her face. In fact, it was Darryl who reminded her, "Aunt Danny, you have to think positive thoughts."

We got into the car and Darryl held me while Mom drove. She drove so fast that she didn't even stop for a light that was red. When we got to the hospital, it was very crowded but an attendant took one look at me and called for someone to rush us to the back room. By this time, I had almost passed out. I was having trouble breathing. I felt numb all over.

The doctor came in quickly. She was a little like Mom. She had long curly dark hair and a big smile. She picked me up and said, "You don't feel too well, do you, sweetie?" She was kind and spoke in a calm, soft voice. I knew that she would take good care of me.

"I need to take Truffles' temperature and then I want to get some X-rays of his lungs. I will take him to the back and you can wait here, if you like."

Mom insisted on coming with me. "I don't want to leave him. Please. Do you mind if we stay with him?" The doctor could see that she was really frightened so she let Mom and Darryl stay with me. Next thing I knew, I was having my temperature taken again, but this time I was too weak to object.

The doctor told Mom that I had a dangerously high fever and that I was very dehydrated. She looked worried but spoke in a way that reassured us. By this time, I was close to passing out. Mom picked me up and held me for a moment and I heard the beat of her heart. That sound gave me strength. I had to get better. What would she do without me? She needed me as much as I needed her. And what about Darryl? I could hear him sobbing. "I love you, Truffles. I'll be right here waiting for you." He sounded so scared. I was not going to give up.

Mom kissed me. "You're my sweet little Truffy. Darryl and I are going to pray for you."

They went into another room to wait. Hours passed and even though I was being prodded and poked and stuck with needles, I knew that they were trying to help me. Still, I was exhausted and I didn't want to be brave any longer. I wanted my mom. I kept looking toward the door, hoping she would come in. Where was she?

I was exhausted and I didn't want to be brave any longer. I wanted my mom.

At that very moment, she came through the door, saying, "I can't stay out there any longer. Truffles is scared and I need to be with him."

The doctor could see it would be impossible to keep her

out, so she let Mom stay with me. Once again I felt safe. Mom leaned over, holding me close and rubbing my ears. As soon as she touched me, I felt calm. She always knew where I liked to be touched. I looked up at her and she was smiling, even though there were tears running down her cheeks. I wanted to lick them and make her feel better, but I couldn't move.

It was already light outside. Mom looked so tired. Her face was pale and her eyes were red from crying. Darryl had fallen asleep on the bench in the waiting room. One of the nurses had given him a blanket and a pillow. They were all so kind and caring at that clinic.

The doctor came into the waiting room with my X-rays. She put them up on the wall and explained what was going on. "Truffles is a very sick puppy. He has pneumonia and his right lung has collapsed. I would like to keep him here for a few days to make sure he gets enough fluids."

Mom's knees started to buckle and she had to sit down. The doctor brought her a cool cloth to put on her forehead. "I can't leave him. He will die without someone to hold him all night. You are wonderful here but you can't stay with him and take care of him the way I will. Just tell me what I have to do and I'll do it."

The doctor agreed that I would be better off at home as long as I was given enough fluids. I was so relieved when I heard her say that I was going to go home with my mom.

"Make sure he is warm. He must drink every two hours, around the clock. That is the most important thing. Try to get him to eat. Boil some chicken and rice and hand feed him little bits at a time. I will give you some meds for him to take three times a day. The first forty-eight hours are crucial."

The doctor said to call her the next day to let her know how I was doing. Mom hugged her and thanked her for being so understanding. I managed to give the doctor's face a lick or two. She had a nice heartbeat and salty skin. I liked her.

By the time we got home, I had fallen asleep. Mom had me wrapped up in a blanket to keep me warm and Darryl was sound asleep in the back seat. Mom woke him up and he went

Mom was worn out. She had a very hard job ahead of her. We both did.

into the house and got right back in bed. Mom was worn out. She had a very hard job ahead of her. We both did. I vowed to do my part by drinking as much as I could every two hours so she could rest in between without worrying so much. I took a few sips and we got into bed and slept.

Darryl went home in the morning. Mom told him that he could come back in a few days. She explained to him that I needed to rest. "Truffles loves you very much, but he gets too excited when he sees you and he has to be very quiet for a while now. I'm sure he will miss playing with you but he will be better soon."

Darryl understood how important this was. He kissed me goodbye and asked if he could call me on the phone. Mom told him that I would love that, and that it was a great idea. I could see that she was smiling when she said it.

I loved lying on pillows. I especially loved rolling around on her bed and rubbing my nose into all the pillows she had there.

Mom brought me upstairs and put me on a heating pad that was under a very soft pillow. I loved lying on pillows. I especially loved rolling around on her bed and rubbing my nose into all the pillows she had there. She had so many of them. It was my favorite place to be, next to being in her arms, but now I didn't feel like doing much of anything. Every time I coughed, and that was a lot of times, it hurt. I was shaking and felt very weak.

"Truffles, you have to drink this or you will die!" Mom kept dripping water into my mouth but I was too weak to swallow so it would just dribble out. She picked me up and held me close to her heart. I could hear it beating so fast. She was crying. "Please, Truffy. I waited so long to find you and I want you to try very hard. Please!"

Mom cancelled all her plans so she could stay with me around the clock. I was scared that I was going to be too much trouble. But she stayed with me day after day. I owed her so much. I was not going to disappoint her. I would fight with every ounce of strength in my body to get well.

"Could this be possible?"

Chapter 5
A Surprise Reunion

As time passed, I started to get stronger. My appetite improved, although I still wasn't eating as much as Mom would have liked. Mom took advantage of all the hours we spent together in the house to teach me a lot of tricks. I must be really smart, just like she says, because I learned everything I was supposed to learn, and quickly. I wanted to make sure she would always be glad that she had chosen me, even after I had been so much trouble.

She kept telling me what a good puppy I am, and I am a good puppy! I never make mistakes on the carpet any more. I know how to roll over, beg, shake hands, crawl on my belly like a soldier, and of course I can fetch. My best trick, though, was learning a signal to let Mom know I had to go out. My signal was that I would grab her leg or shoe with my teeth and shake my head.

Darryl was coming to see me nearly every day again. Even before the doorbell rang, I knew that he was outside. I would bark and wag my tail, waiting for the door to open.

As soon as he came in, I would roll over so he could tickle me and rub my belly. This was becoming one of my favorite things. He would get on the floor and play with me for hours. Mom even let him take me on the leash and walk me up and down the block.

When we went for our walks, I would often notice

Something about his bark made me realize how much I wanted to have a friend to run around with.

a dog at the window of a house down the street, poking his head through some curtains. I could hear him barking at me, but all I could see was the top of his head. Something about his bark made me realize how much I wanted to have a friend to run around with. I so missed playing with Tanner. Maybe when

I was all better, the barking dog would come out and play with me.

I still had a little infection in my lungs so Mom was extra careful not to let me do too much. To tell the truth, she was overprotective of me but I didn't mind because I knew I was getting stronger every day.

"Truffles! Truffles! Where are you, Monkey Face? We have to go to the doctor now."

Mom was taking me for a checkup to see if my lungs were clear. I hoped I was all better so I could run and play outside like the other dogs.

This time when we got to the doctor's office, it was during the day and there were so many dogs there. They were shaking and whimpering and carrying on like such babies. I was the smallest one there, and I wasn't shaking, I was brave. Besides, I liked it there. I remembered how everyone had helped me and treated me with kindness.

When the doctor saw me, she got down on the floor to talk to me. "You look much, much better, little guy. Your mom sure took good care of you!" She picked me up and gave me a big hug. Then she put me on the scale. I had gained one-quarter of a pound. That was very good. Then out came the dreaded thermometer. Why? I didn't have a fever! I felt perfectly fine! But before I could protest, up went my tail and in went the thermometer.

"Everything looks great so far. His temp is normal and he has a very strong heartbeat." The doctor looked pleased and I was also happy to hear the good news.

Mom was so happy she teared up. Poor Mom. She had shed a lot of tears over me in our short time together. But at least these were the happy tears again. "Thank God! I just couldn't bear to hear anything bad."

The doctor wanted to take another X-ray to make sure my lungs were better. "If all is well, you can stop the meds and forget Truffles was ever sick."

She picked me up to take me to the back room. Mom waited outside this time. She knew I would be fine going there on my own.

Everyone in back seemed thrilled to see me. They were all smiling and petting me while the doctor X-rayed my lungs. One technician was so happy that I hadn't died that he started clapping his hands, then hugged me. "You made it, little guy."

The doctor picked me up, brought me back out to my mom, and gave me a big kiss on the top of my head as she handed me over to her. "Take your precious baby home and have a good life. He's perfect!" She shook Mom's hand, gave me a treat and said goodbye.

My luck had returned. No more doctors and no more pills. I could finally go outside and play, like the big dogs.

We got back in the car. Mom was elated. Instead of

going right home, she stopped off at this place called Starbucks. There were lots of people there with their dogs. There were many tables and chairs outside and loads of kids running around. This was my first real outing and I was so excited. Mom picked me up and slipped me into her purse to take me inside. There was a long line of people waiting for coffee. Everyone seemed to know Mom. They asked where she had been lately and she told them how sick I'd been and how she'd been at home nursing me.

I have to say, people went kind of nuts when they saw me. Especially the children.

I have to say, people went kind of nuts when they saw me. Especially the children. There were children reaching for me, left and right. They thought I was a little stuffed animal at first and they squealed with delight when they saw that I was a real dog. I really liked all the attention. There was something about the children that I especially liked. I felt a connection with them, just as I had when I first met Darryl.

"What an adorable puppy you have." "Can I pet your dog?" "What's his name?" "Where did you get him?" "He's such an interesting color." And that old standard, "Is it a boy or a girl?" The questions kept coming and Mom was beaming with pride. She always loved showing me off, and she allowed everyone to pet me, but she didn't let anyone hold me. She was afraid I would be dropped and break a leg or something, I guess. After all, I still only weighed less than two pounds and I was pretty fragile.

After Mom got her coffee, we went outside and she sat down at a table. I snuggled into her lap and went to sleep. Something about being in her lap always made me fall asleep right away.

While she drank her coffee and I slept, a man came over to us. He was staring at me so intently that Mom reacted and I woke up. He had a look of amazement on his face. "Do you know, I have a puppy at home that looks exactly like yours? I mean, exactly! I thought this one was mine for a minute."

He was a handsome man, with a nice smile and white teeth. He wore his hair all slicked back and had a deep tan. He told Mom that she looked familiar to him, but he couldn't figure out how he knew her. The funny thing was that he looked familiar to me, too. My tail started wagging as fast as if I remembered how I knew him. I was sure excited to see him, whoever he was.

He asked Mom where she had gotten me. When Mom told him that I came from Laguna, in southern California, he exclaimed, "You're kidding! That's where we got our puppy."

"I got Truffles from Patsy's Puppies." Mom had hardly finished saying this when the man exclaimed, "You've got to be kidding! We got our dog from Patsy's, too! This is just too weird."

By this time they were both laughing. I wasn't exactly sure what all the excitement was about but I couldn't help but be excited, too. Mom and the man, who said his name was Richard, continued comparing notes. When Mom heard that his dog was also born in August, she gasped. "They are the same age and come from the same place. Oh, my God! Is it possible that they're brothers?"

Richard picked up his cell phone and called his wife. I heard him say, "Honey, you must come down to Starbucks right away. Don't ask questions. Just come." He went on to say something else to his wife, but just then someone knocked over a cup of coffee and caused a commotion so I couldn't hear what it was.

"Honey, you must come down to Starbucks right away. Don't ask questions. Just come."

While we waited for Richard's wife, Tanya, to show up, Mom fed me a treat and gave me some water. I was now eating hard food and I didn't get many tummy aches any more. Mom said she couldn't wait to meet Tanya and their dog and I was thinking how nice it would be if he turned out to be a friend I could play with.

It wasn't long before Tanya drove up in a bright yellow Jeep. She had long red hair and, like Richard, looked somehow familiar to me. She walked over to us, holding a dog in her arms. When she saw me, her eyes widened and her mouth opened. "I can't believe this! They're twins!"

Sure enough, the dog she was holding looked exactly like me! Tanya put him down and as I finally got a good look at him, my heart started racing. Could this be possible? I jumped up and started barking and yipping.

It was Tanner! He looked at me and then we started running as fast as we could toward each other. We were both yelping excitedly and we ran around each other in circles, giving each other little love bites. He jumped on me, holding me down with his paws, and I licked his face. I had never really expected to see my best friend again. We played and played until we were exhausted. Then we lay down together on my blanket, licking and nuzzling each other, just as we had done so long ago.

While Tanner and I were running around, our parents sat at the table, laughing and talking as they watched us. They couldn't get over how their two puppies were reacting to each other. As they talked, Mom and Richard discovered that they had known each other years ago, when they both lived in New York City, and that Mom had also known his parents and his sister there. Now that their whole family was in California, Mom said she couldn't wait to see them again, after so many years had gone by. They also discovered that they lived only a few minutes away from each other, so it would be easy to get together. This news made me happiest of all. It looked like Tanner and I would be able to see each other often.

After a couple of hours, everyone got up to leave. They hugged each other and then they exchanged kisses. Tanner and I were hugged and kissed, too. Richard took a picture of the two of us on his cell phone. We licked and licked each other goodbye but this time we knew it wouldn't be for forever.

Chapter 6
Time for School

The next morning, Mom took me out for a long walk. We loved going out in the early morning when the air was cool and the birds were waking up and chirping their morning songs. The fresh smells in the crisp air started each day off just right.

I was allowed to walk without my leash because I never ran away, unlike some of the other dogs. Even if I saw a cat or a bird or a squirrel I would stay by Mom's side until she gave me permission to go. But for some reason, on this particular day, Mom put my leash on. I protested, but she put it on me anyway.

There was this big cat that lived next door to us. He sat on a front step all day and basked in the sun. The first time I went over to him, he crouched down and hissed at me but soon we were rubbing noses and I never got scratched. We understood each other. The truth is, I liked everyone— even the rabbits on the grass, who always ran away from me— and everyone seemed to like me. I was just a happy, grateful puppy.

While we were on our way home from our walk that morning, a big yellow dog jumped out of the bushes and ran straight toward me. After I got over being surprised, I wanted to play with him but as soon as she saw him, Mom started to scream hysterically. She yanked me up by the leash and I landed, topsy-turvy, in her arms. She was shouting, "Get away! Get away! Scram!" and waving her free arm frantically.

A neighbor ran out of her house, holding her own little dog, the dog that always barked as we passed by. "What's wrong? Are you okay?" She came over to us, looking concerned.

By this time, Mom was squeezing me so tightly that I could hardly breathe. She was shaking and crying. "Coyote, there's a coyote! He attacked us! I can't believe he almost got Truffles."

Mom sat down on the grass, still holding onto me. The girl bent over and put her arms around Mom, trying to calm her down. "I hear the coyotes at night but I never thought they would come right up to anyone, especially during the daytime. I am never taking Sailor out without a leash again. Are you sure you're okay?"

"Coyote, there's a coyote! He attacked us! I can't believe he almost got Truffles."

She was so nice that Mom relaxed and soon started to laugh. "I can't believe I freaked out like that. But if anything ever happened to Truffles, I would absolutely die!"

The girl started to laugh, too. In a few minutes, they were talking and getting to know each other.

"My name is Sophia, what's yours?"

Mom introduced herself and then introduced me. Sophia bent down and put her dog Sailor's nose next to mine, to see if we would like each other. It turned out that she wasn't a boy, like I'd always thought. Not at all. She was a beautiful girl and she smelled really good. Both our tails were wagging furiously so I could tell that she liked me, too.

Mom invited Sophia in for coffee. They talked for a long time. Sophia worked as a fundraiser for a charity that granted wishes for children with life-threatening diseases. Mom told her about the pet therapy program she'd started several years ago called Tender Loving Zoo or TLZ. She explained that it was a non-profit organization that brought animals to convalescent homes for the elderly and to children with physical and mental challenges. Mom told Sophia that I would soon be

"I'm going to get Truffles certified as a therapy dog one of these days. He'll be great."

working with her. "I'm going to get Truffles certified as a therapy dog one of these days. He'll be great."

That was news to me. I had no idea what a therapy dog was, but it sounded important because Mom's voice got real serious when she talked about it, and if she thought I'd be great at it, I was eager to find out what it was and give it a try.

My six months birthday party was coming up soon and Mom invited Sophia and Sailor to come. I was getting pretty big. I weighed almost three and a half pounds and my legs were just long enough so that I could make it up and down the stairs without falling backward or forward.

Mom had thrown a party for me every month since I had come to live with her. Richard and Tanya brought Tanner to our house to celebrate our monthly birthdays together. Other members of Mom's family came, too, and lots of her friends. Everyone would snap pictures and have such a good time. I would beg, roll over, shake hands, speak and do whatever else Mom had taught me to do.

Every month Tanner and I couldn't wait to dive into my birthday cake. It looked like chocolate but it was made from carob. I heard Mom telling Darryl that I could die if I ate real chocolate because chocolate is very bad for dogs. So instead we would have a yummy carob cake, covered with milk bones.

Six months must be a very important birthday because so many more people came to my party than usual. Everyone brought presents but instead of giving them to me, they put them under this big green tree that Mom had brought in from outside and had standing in the living room. She'd put all kinds of things on its branches—crystal balls and bells and figures and lots of candy canes. There were even some photos hanging from it. One of me, of course, and one of Darryl and me, and Mom and me, and one of the whole

I love carob birthday cake!

"I'm one year old!"

family, including me. There was also a picture of Richard and Tanya, holding Tanner. There were lights that blinked on and off and lit up the whole room like the stars in the night sky. There was a big crystal star on the top of the tree. It sparkled like a diamond and it was Mom's favorite piece. She told people that her father had given it to her when she was a little girl and she had kept it all these years and it was very precious to her.

When Sophia and Sailor came in, Tanner and I ran over to Sailor and I introduced her to Tanner by sniffing her first. I thought she was going to start barking at Tanner, the way she used to bark at me from her window, but she didn't. Sophia couldn't believe that Sailor was being so good but she seemed to like Tanner a lot, probably because he looked so much like me.

Sophia picked me up and gave me a birthday kiss. Then she unwrapped my present for me. It was a big, soft, fluffy bed. Sailor had the same bed and I had jumped into it when we had gone to her house so Sophia thought I would like to have one of my own. She was right. I loved it and gave her lots of licks to say thank you. I was so happy with it that I didn't mind that a lot of the presents under the tree didn't seem to be for me.

Not long after my party, Mom said she thought it was time for me to go to school. Hmm, I thought, I already know everything and I am never less than perfectly behaved, so why do I have to go to school? But it turned out that the school was not for obedience training. It was a place where dogs learned to become certified as therapy dogs.

When we arrived, I got pretty excited. There were lots of dogs there—big yellow dogs and big black dogs, mostly—though none that were little, like me. Once we got signed in, I went around exchanging sniffs with the other dogs. Everyone liked me, except for one dog, and he was asked to leave since he didn't get along with anyone.

After a few more minutes, each dog was asked to sit by his or her owner and just be quiet while the teacher described what we had to do to earn our diploma. Then we were told to sit on one side of the room while our owners went to the other side. No one was allowed to move until we were called, one by one. It was easy for me to wait, as I always did, until my Mom called me to come to her, but most of the other dogs ran to their owners right away, way before being called.

Next we had to walk around and say hello to everyone who was sitting in the circle. As long as no one growled or showed their teeth, they were allowed to stay, even if their man-

> *As long as no one growled or showed their teeth, they were allowed to stay, even if their manners weren't perfect.*

ners weren't perfect. This part was fun for me because I love making new friends. There were a few children there and when I got to them, I was so pleased to meet them that I jumped up and down and started licking them. I thought I might be scolded for doing that but then I saw that the teacher was smiling at me, and Mom picked me up and kissed me so I guessed it was all right to make a fuss over the children.

The teacher put a bowl of treats down on the floor and each dog was given one, one at a time. The test was whether or not the dog would let the teacher take away the treat once the dog started eating it. A few of the dogs growled, and they flunked right away. When it was my turn, I took the treat in my mouth and then gave it back to the teacher. She didn't know it, but at home, whenever anyone came to visit, I would run and fetch a toy or one of my treats to take to the visitor, as a present. The teacher started to laugh, along with everyone there. She told Mom that there was no way I wouldn't be getting a diploma. "Truffles is so smart and sweet and gentle. He doesn't bark at the other dogs or show any aggression at all. He'll make a wonderful therapy dog."

After an hour, the class was over, and of course I passed. I was given a bright orange jacket that said "Therapy Dog" on it, and I got to wear it home. I still wasn't sure what it all meant, but I knew I'd made my mom proud, and that's what I try to do all the time.

I love you, Olivia.

Chapter 7

A Purpose Found

The next morning I was all snuggled up next to Mom when the alarm went off. Usually Mom and I just stay in bed until I'm awake enough to go out for our walk. First I give myself a big stretch, then a nice big yawn, and then I lick Mom's face to wake her up. She always pretends she's still asleep, but I know she's faking it. It's a game we've played ever since I came to live with her. Next, she pops out of bed, throws some cold water on her face, grabs a sweater to put on over her jeans and takes me outside for a good long walk. She likes getting up early. To her, it's a waste of time to sleep the mornings away.

But this was obviously a special morning. She took out my brush and fluffed me all up. Then she brushed my teeth, as she does five times a week. (She has this thing about beautiful, white teeth.)

A little later she drove us to this enormous house that was set way back from the street. There were huge orange trees lining the driveway. Beautiful flowers surrounded the entire entrance to the home. It looked like a happy place.

Mom parked the car. I was all ready to hop out but she sat for a long time before opening the door. Finally, she got out and put me on the ground, then popped open the trunk of the car and took out a bunch of presents that were all gift-wrapped with shiny paper and sparkly ribbons.

… when the door opened, standing in front of us were five people–two grownups and three children–with completely bald heads.

We walked up to the door and rang the bell and when the door opened, standing in front of us were five people—two grownups and three children— with completely bald heads. I was so surprised I didn't even bark at them but Mom didn't seem surprised at all.

They all greeted each other like family. I soon learned that the children's mother, Stephanie, had been Mom's best friend since elementary school. Mom and Stephanie kept hugging and seemed very happy to see one another. So why were they crying? If these were happy tears, they must have been very happy because there were an awful lot of tears. I was a little confused, so I just stood still and wagged my tail and watched what was happening.

Stephanie led Mom and me into a bedroom, where they sat on the bed, holding hands and talking softly about another child of Stephanie's, whom I hadn't yet met. She was resting in another room, Stephanie told Mom. Mom was saying, "She was so healthy a few months ago. It's so hard to believe. What can I do for her? I feel so helpless."

Stephanie shook her head. They both cried some more, then a while later they were both laughing, about the silliest things. Mom seemed to be able to make anyone laugh, even at things that weren't funny. I burrowed into her lap and tried to make myself even smaller than I am while they talked and talked.

Suddenly Mom said she had an idea. "I'm going to shave my head like the rest of you. If it makes Olivia feel a little better, then it's worth doing. Where's a razor?"

"No, wait a minute. Think about it. Are you sure you want to look like a Martian?" Stephanie asked, her voice getting all serious.

"Yes, I'm absolutely sure. Besides, I need a haircut and this will save me a trip to the hairdresser."

Stephanie gave Mom the biggest hug yet, then called to her oldest daughter to bring in an electric razor and do the honors. When she came in, Mom took a deep breath, then said, "Wait, let me put my hair in a ponytail first so I can donate it to someone who might need it."

As Mom's beautiful hair fell to the ground, she began to

cry again, but it turned out she wasn't crying about losing her hair. "How could God do this to Olivia? Of all the people in the world, why your beautiful daughter?"

Stephanie put her arm around Mom's shoulders. "Danny, you have to listen to what Olivia has to say about that. Somehow she has the strength that I'm supposed to have. That is what God gave her. He gave her the strength to get through this. Please don't give up your faith. Olivia needs you to believe and have hope."

Mom nodded. I could tell that she was not going to give up on Olivia. She got up and twirled around. Her beautiful long hair was all gone. I guess she looked pretty funny but she was still my mom so she looked fine to me. "All right, let's go. It's time for the unveiling!"

When she walked into the living room, the rest of the family cheered. Then everyone was hugging her and thanking her. I began to wonder if giving up my chocolate coat would make a difference and if people would cheer if all my beautiful fur curls were shaved off. But that thought didn't seem to occur to anyone else. After a while, Mom told Stephanie that she was ready to see Olivia in her room, alone—except for me, of course.

We walked down the hall and opened a closed door. Olivia was lying in bed, entirely bald and looking very pale and quiet, but beautiful nonetheless. When we came in, she sat up and stared at Mom's shaved head, speechless. She really did not say a single word for a whole minute! And then she exclaimed, "Aunt Danny, you are the best! I love you so much. I can't believe you did this for me."

She began to laugh and cry at the same time, just like Mom and Stephanie had earlier, and then suddenly she noticed me, tucked under Mom's arm. "Oh, my God! Where did you get this adorable puppy? He's so tiny!"

She stretched out her arms to me. Mom brought me

over to the bed and handed me to Olivia, very carefully. I could sense how frail and tired Olivia was, in spite of her enthusiasm. I remembered that in my training as a therapy dog it had been all right to jump up and lick the children but I sensed this was a different situation. When Olivia held me to her chest, I could tell by her heartbeat that I needed to be still and just let her cuddle me and keep me close. I realized that there is a time and place for being

> *When Olivia held me to her chest, I could tell by her heartbeat that I needed to be still and just let her cuddle me and keep me close.*

quiet and a time and place for jumping around and playing and it was up to me to figure out which was which when I was on the job.

This was my time to be there for Olivia. Instead of doing what I usually do when I meet new people, especially children—barking and leaping about and making them laugh at my antics—I just lay quietly in her arms and allowed her to pet me. Of course I licked her a little (well, more than a little, actually), but I could tell that that was okay to do. After all, I was just returning her kisses.

After spending an hour with Olivia, and seeing how happy she seemed to be that I was there with her, I thought I really understood what being a therapy dog meant. I was already looking forward to the next time Mom would put my orange therapy jacket on me. Because now I know that when that happens, it won't be long before I'll be making someone's day a little brighter, while also pleasing the person who means the very most to me, my mom!

About the Authors

Truffles continues to provide love and lick therapy to those who need special attention. **Nancy Stanley**, a former New Yorker, has been recognized as one of the modern day Animal Therapy Pioneers. She first introduced "Animal Therapy" to severly handicapped children and to convalescent hospitals for the elderly in 1982 after Founding Tender Loving Zoo, a nonprofit organization. Nancy also served as the National Media and Public Relations Director of Tender Loving Zoo. Nancy is a Mother, Grandmother and a wish-grantor for the Make-A-Wish-Foundation. She lives by the ocean in Carlsbad, California.

Published by Journey Publishing
P.O. Box 131554 • Carlsbad, Ca. 92013 • 760-420-7171
www.Pillowwithaheartbeat.com

Edited by Nancy Hardin

Printed through Four Colour Print Group, Louisville, KY 40206.
ISBN: 978-0-9817069-1-7